I'm Reading About

JAMESTOWN

by Carole Marsh

Photo Credits: Cover and Pages 11A, 13, 15, 20, 24, 26, 30, 34A: National Park Service, Colonial National Historical Park, Jamestown Collection. Page 5: Henry William Powell, Architect of the Capitol. Page 9: Seaman Matthew Bookwalter, U.S. Navy. Page 11B: NOAA. Page 14: Nationalparks at en.wikipedia CC BY-SA 2.5. Page 17A: Morgan Riley, wikimedia.org; 17B: STC 22790, Houghton Library, Harvard University. Page 18A: National Park Service, Colonial National Historical Park (Robin Baranowski, NPS Photo); 18B: Sarah Stierch CC BY-SA 2.0. Page 22: Library of Congress. Page 28: Wellcome Images CC BY 4.0. Page 32A: Smithsonian Institution CC BY-SA 3.0; 32B: Smash the Iron Cage CC BY-SA 4.0. Page 34B: sainaniritu/Bigstock.com.

Jamestown is an important place in American history!

What is so special about Jamestown?

Let's read about it and see!

COLONIZATION

In the 1500s and 1600s, Spain and France set up colonies in the New World. Why were colonies important?

★They provided new land to control.

★They provided resources like wood from trees.

★They provided new places for trade.

In short, colonies provided increased riches!

Colonies were also a way to spread the Christian religion.

New Colonies

In the 1500s, England decided to start
colonies in the New World, too.

In 1585, English colonists settled on Roanoke Island
in present–day North Carolina.
The colonists could not survive there and returned home.

In 1587, John White led more settlers to Roanoke.
He sailed back to England for supplies.
When he returned to the colony, everyone was gone!
Today, Roanoke is called the "Lost Colony."

Roanoke Island

FIRST ENGLISH
COLONIES
Explored in 1584. Site of
first English settlements
in new world, 1585-1587.
Birthplace of Virginia
Dare, first child born of
English parents in America.

In 1606, King James I of England decided to try again!
He allowed the Virginia Company of London
to start a colony in America.

In December, about 100 colonists sailed
from England to present-day Virginia.
Their three ships were named
the *Susan Constant*, the *Godspeed*, and the *Discovery*.

Their journey took five long months!

Jamestown
was founded in
May 1607.

That was
more than 400
years ago!

Jamestown
Landing

The colonists named their new settlement "Jamestown." They chose a spot far inland and along a river because:

⭐ The river was deep enough for their ships.

⭐ They could spot enemy ships coming toward them.

⭐ Water on three sides made it easier to defend.

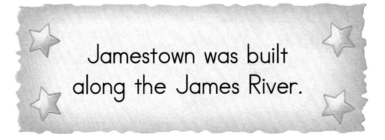

Jamestown was built along the James River.

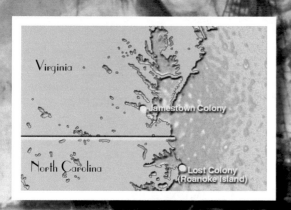

Virginia

Jamestown Colony

North Carolina

Lost Colony
(Roanoke Island)

New Settlement

FORT

The colonists knew they had to have a safe home.
They built a wooden fort shaped like a triangle.
Each corner had a raised area for cannons.

Buildings inside the fort included a
storehouse, church, and houses.
The houses were made of wood and clay.
Usually six to eight men lived in each house.

We could have lived there!

We don't take up much room.

Safe Fort

Thousands of Powhatan Indians lived around Jamestown.
Their chief was known as "Chief Powhatan."
He ruled more than 30 tribes.
He was very powerful!

The Powhatan Indians were farmers.
They feared the colonists would take their land.
Sometimes they helped the colonists,
and sometimes they attacked them.

The Powhatan Indians lived in
houses called " yehakins."

Powhatan Indians

WORK

Life in Jamestown was very hard.
There was a LOT of work to be done,
like farming, hunting, and building.

But many of the colonists were English " gentlemen "
who had never done hard work.

Captain John Smith was the leader of the colony.
He was angry at the men who did not work.
He told them, "If you don't work, you don't eat!"

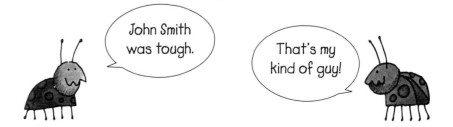

John Smith was tough.

That's *my* kind of guy!

Hard Work

THE PORTRAICTVER OF CAPTAYNE IOHN SMITH ADMIRALL OF NEW ENGLAND.

Et at: 37
A° 1616

Of Salvages, much Civilliz'd by thee

Captain John Smith

Salt Marsh

Graves in Jamestown

Poor Location

The colonists soon realized that Jamestown's location was not as good as they had thought.
The land was marshy and wet.
That caused many problems:

⭐ Many crops did not grow well in the soil.

⭐ Drinking the river water made people sick.

⭐ Insects in the swampy land spread disease.

More than half of the colonists died in the first year.

PROBLEMS

Trading Goods

How did Jamestown survive that first year?
The colonists traded goods with the Powhatan Indians.

John Smith talked to the Indians.
He offered things the Indians wanted
like glass beads, copper, and iron tools.

In return, the Indians traded much-needed food
to the starving, desperate colonists.

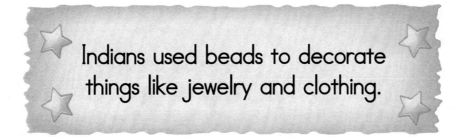

Indians used beads to decorate
things like jewelry and clothing.

TRADE

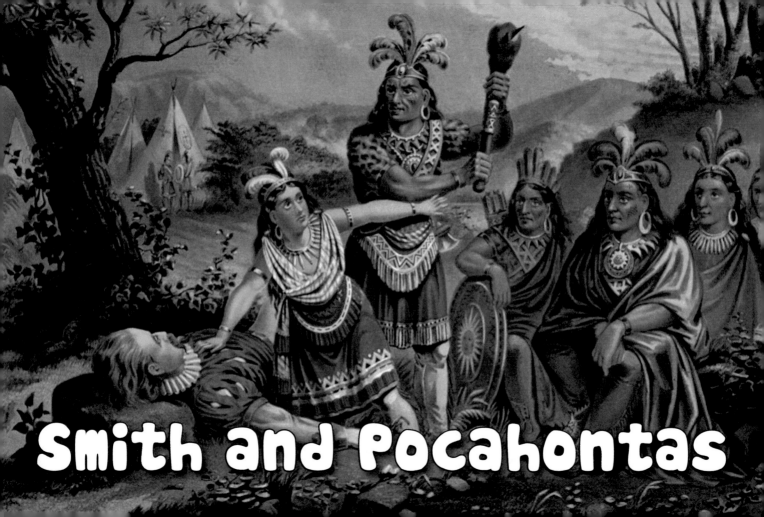

Smith and Pocahontas

John Smith often explored the area around Jamestown.
One day, the Powhatan Indians captured him!
He was taken to Chief Powhatan.

Smith described what happened to him:

He said the Indians laid him on the ground.
He thought they were going to kill him.
Chief Powhatan's daughter Pocahontas
put her head over his body to save his life!

Pocahontas liked to visit Jamestown.

She was curious about the colonists!

POCAHONTAS

Starving Time

With John Smith's leadership, things improved in Jamestown.
More people came from England to settle in the colony.
But in 1609, Smith was injured in a gunpowder explosion.
He had to return to England for medical help.

The winter after John Smith left was a terrible time.
The Indians and colonists were not getting along.
Colonists were afraid to leave the fort and had little food.
It was known as the "Starving Time."

During the Starving Time,
about 80% of the colonists died.

TRAGEDY

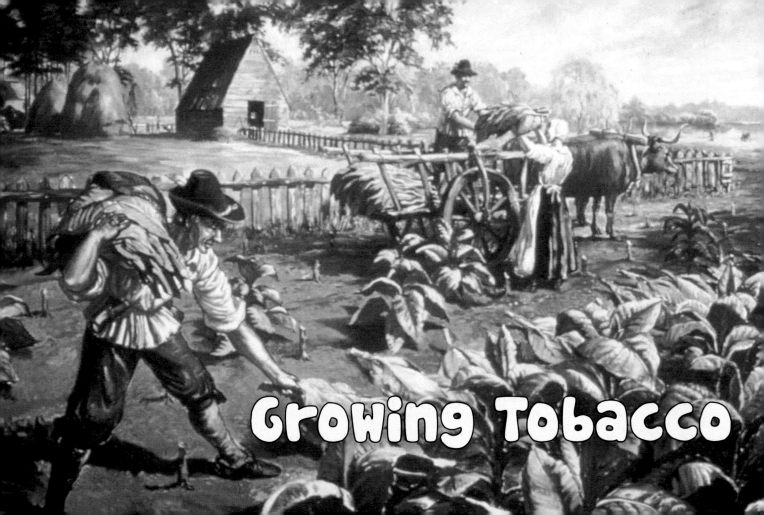

Growing Tobacco

Survivors of the Starving Time decided to leave Jamestown.
But they changed their minds when new colonists
and much-needed supplies arrived.
Jamestown would go on!

John Rolfe was one of the new settlers.
He showed the colonists how to plant a new crop—tobacco.
Tobacco grew well in the Virginia soil.
The colonists sent tobacco to England to sell.

Tobacco gave
the colony a way to
make money.

You gotta
have some cash,
you know!

TOBACCO

Pocahontas Marries

The colonists needed more land to grow tobacco.
They began taking more land around Jamestown.
The Powhatan Indians fought to keep their land.
They killed settlers and set fire to the colonists' homes.

In 1614, a time of peace came to the region
when John Rolfe married Pocahontas!
The colonists had kidnapped her in 1613.
She had learned English ways while in Jamestown.

Pocahontas took an English name—
Rebecca.

Indians Attack

The time of peace between the Indians and colonists
only lasted for about 8 years.
The Powhatan Indians got tired of the colonists
taking their land—and attacked again!

Fighting continued, off and on, for decades.
Finally, the colonists took all the lands around Jamestown.

Jamestown grew into a successful community.
It was the capital of Virginia for many years!

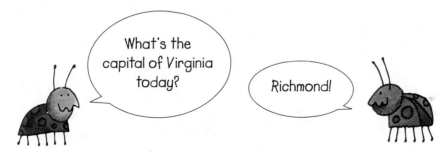

What's the capital of Virginia today?

Richmond!

NO PEACE

James Fort Remains

Skeletons Found

Building Ruins

Many people thought the Jamestown fort had washed away. They were wrong! In 1994, archaeologists began to uncover remains of the fort.

Today, you can see objects from the colony in a museum located in Historic Jamestowne:

⭐ helmets, breastplates, and weapons

⭐ musical instruments and dice

⭐ pottery, dishes, coins, and buttons

Historic Jamestowne is part of Colonial National Historical Park.

ARTIFACTS

First Lasting Settlement

Jamestown was the first permanent
English settlement in America!
Read more fascinating facts about it:

⭐ The first women came to Jamestown in 1608.

⭐ Pocahontas was about 12 years old when she met John Smith.

⭐ Settlers even ate shoes and boots during the Starving Time.

⭐ The first Africans arrived in Jamestown in 1619.

⭐ Over one million artifacts have been discovered at James Fort!

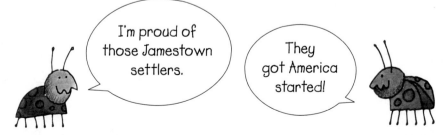

I'm proud of those Jamestown settlers.

They got America started!

DID YOU KNOW?

GLOSSARY

archaeologist: a person who studies artifacts to learn how people lived in the past

artifact: an object made and used by humans in the past

colony: a distant territory belonging to or under the control of a nation

decade: a period of ten years

desperate: beyond or almost beyond hope

inland: located in a place away from the ocean or open water

kidnap: to take someone away against their will

tobacco: a plant with leaves that are smoked in cigarettes and pipes